Great Buddhists of the Twentieth Century

Also by Sangharakshita

A Survey of Buddhism
The Three Jewels
Mind – Reactive and Creative
The Essence of Zen
Peace is a Fire
The Thousand-Petalled Lotus (*memoirs*)
Human Enlightenment
The Religion of Art
The Ten Pillars of Buddhism
The Eternal Legacy
Travel Letters
Going for Refuge
Alternative Traditions
Who is the Buddha?
The Meaning of Orthodoxy in Buddhism
Ambedkar and Buddhism
A Guide to the Buddhist Path
Crossing the Stream
The History of My Going for Refuge
The Taste of Freedom
Vision and Transformation
Learning to Walk (*memoirs*)
New Currents in Western Buddhism
My Relation to the Order
The Buddha's Victory
Facing Mount Kanchenjunga (*memoirs*)
Buddhism and the West
The Priceless Jewel
The Drama of Cosmic Enlightenment
The FWBO and 'Protestant Buddhism'
Wisdom Beyond Words
Forty-Three Years Ago
The Meaning of Conversion in Buddhism
Complete Poems 1941–1994
Was the Buddha a Bhikkhu?
In the Realm of the Lotus
Transforming Self and World
Buddhism for Today – and Tomorrow
Ritual and Devotion in Buddhism
The Inconceivable Emancipation
In the Sign of the Golden Wheel (*memoirs*)
Extending the Hand of Fellowship

GREAT BUDDHISTS OF THE TWENTIETH CENTURY

SANGHARAKSHITA

WINDHORSE PUBLICATIONS

Published by Windhorse Publications
Unit 1-316 The Custard Factory
Gibb Street
Birmingham
B9 4AA

© Sangharakshita 1996

Printed by Colbourne & Underwood
2 Lower Trinity Street
Birmingham
B9 4AA

Typesetting Sue Parker
Cover design Annie Moss

The cover shows the rupa in the main shrine-room of Sukhavati community, designed by Chintamani, photographed by Silabhadra

British Library Cataloguing in Publication Data
A catalogue record for this book is available from the British Library

ISBN 0 904766 80 2

PUBLISHER'S NOTE: Since this work is intended for a general readership, Pali and Sanskrit words are transliterated without the diacritical marks that would have been appropriate in a work of a more scholarly nature.

Editor's Preface

Sangharakshita's introduction to five key figures in the history of Buddhism in the twentieth century has been published to coincide with the fortieth anniversary of the crowning achievement of one of those five. This was the mass-conversion of ex-Untouchables to Buddhism initiated by Dr Ambedkar on 14 October 1956. It is an anniversary of particular personal significance to Sangharakshita himself, because he was the young English Buddhist monk who continued the conversion movement after Ambedkar's sudden death in the same year.

The pages that follow constitute an edited version of a lecture delivered by Sangharakshita in 1995 on – by an unforeseen but auspicious coincidence – 14 October. The lecture was given under the auspices of the Maha Bodhi Society, which was founded by Dharmapala, the first of Sangharakshita's choice of five great Buddhists. Sangharakshita has a connection with the society going back some fifty years, and edited its organ, the *Maha Bodhi Journal*, for twelve years from 1952.

Sangharakshita was, by his own admission, 'a ferocious editor', ruthlessly blue-pencilling articles submitted for publication with all the confidence of a very young man. However, we have not followed his example in our own editing: we have retained most of the content of the talk, together with something of the style in which it was delivered. We have tried to do the minimum necessary to turn the transcript of a lecture into a booklet.

The choice of subject-matter was not in fact Sangharakshita's own. And he admits that he did not look upon the prospect of tackling it with any immediate relish. However, as he said in his introduction to the talk, 'why not sometimes speak on a subject which is not of one's own choosing? Perhaps it will stretch one a little beyond one's customary boundaries – not to say limitations.'

Certainly, it would be hard to think of anyone alive today who is better qualified to address this subject. Sangharakshita has been taught by distinguished representatives of all the major Buddhist traditions, from a Theravadin bhikkhu to a Ch'an master, and including a number of Tibetan lamas who settled around Kalimpong in northern India where he was living in the 1950s. As a renowned and respected teacher and scholar himself, he has also had contact with – and in some cases enjoyed the friendship of – many other major figures in the Buddhist world.* In the case of all the five outstanding characters he has chosen to highlight, he has a uniquely personal, or at least particularly privileged, view of their lives and work.

Clearly, Sangharakshita could have chosen a completely different set of five great Buddhists of the twentieth century to speak about. What we have here is very much a personal choice. But it is a collection that hangs together. A striking and unifying feature is that all of these individuals ran right against the grain of the particular society in which they grew up. In this their lives were, perhaps, quintessentially twentieth century lives. One has the sense of barriers being broken down, of fresh intellectual territory being opened up. And here they follow a similar pattern to that of Sangharakshita's own life. He began it as an English boy, living in South London, but

---
* See Sangharakshita's memoirs (passim): *The Thousand-Petalled Lotus*.
Alan Sutton, 1988; *Facing Mount Kanchenjunga*, Windhorse, 1991;
In the Sign of the Golden Wheel, Windhorse, 1996.

realized at the age of sixteen, in 1941, that he was a Buddhist 'and always had been'. After that, his life has been a single-minded working out of the implications of that fact.

Sangharakshita could not, of course, very well include himself amongst the great Buddhists of the twentieth century. However, there are thousands of ex-Untouchables in India today who still remember with gratitude how he held together the conversion movement after the shock of the sudden death of Dr Ambedkar threatened to bring it to a halt almost before it had begun. He is also widely regarded as an important figure in the efflorescence of Buddhism in the West in the second half of the century, mainly through his founding of the Friends of the Western Buddhist Order. This organization now has public centres, retreat centres, communities, and right-livelihood businesses throughout the world. It flourishes too amongst the ex-Untouchable community in India (where it is called the Trailokya Bauddha Maha Sahayak Gana) and where it continues Dr Ambedkar's work of providing people with the opportunity to achieve dignity and freedom.* If, therefore, it takes one to know one, then we may say that Sangharakshita can probably speak with some authority on great Buddhists of the modern era.

Jinananda
Spoken Word Project
West London Buddhist Centre
August 1996

---

* See Steven Batchelor: *The Awakening of the West*, HarperCollins, 1994.

Great Buddhists of the Twentieth Century

Hero-worship is not in fashion at this time, at the end of the twentieth century – except, perhaps, in a perverted, degenerate or trivial form. History is nowadays presented – even to children – in terms of the small doings of ordinary people rather than the momentous actions of great individuals. It would appear that children are offered facts and figures – and of course pocket calculators – rather than the inspirational examples of heroes like Nelson and Florence Nightingale. And this does seem to me a very unfortunate development. We need people we can look up to, people on whom we can model ourselves, and from whom we can derive inspiration. We need, in short, heroes in the true, positive sense.

Above all, we need spiritual heroes; and not only heroes – even legendary heroes – from the dim and distant past, but also heroic exemplars from our own time. Nor is there any dearth of contemporary or near-contemporary ones. I have to say that I started turning over in my mind this subject of great Buddhists of the twentieth century with the assumption that there would be no more than a handful of individuals to consider. But it did not take me long to realize that I had a problem. There seemed to have been dozens upon dozens of them.

Unless one is going to attempt an exhaustive guide to the great Buddhists of the twentieth century one has to select. And unless one is going to do this according to mere whim, then one has to look round for some meaningful principles by which to make one's selection. On what basis could I focus on certain individuals and not others?

In the end I allowed two principles to direct my choice. First, I decided not to touch upon any great Buddhists who were still alive. After all, there is always the faint possibility of great Buddhists ceasing to be so, either by changing their religion or by losing their greatness of character – and then where would that leave us? Edward Gibbon remarks that in the later stages of the reign of the emperor Constantine the Great, who was later canonized as St Constantine, 'we may contemplate a hero, who had so long inspired his subjects with love and his enemies with terror, degenerating into a cruel and dissolute monarch...'. So such things happen from time to time, unfortunately. We should heed Sophocles' warning: 'Call no man happy until he is dead,' and be wary of calling someone a great Buddhist too definitively before he or she is safely dead.

As for my second principle of selection, this was to consider no one with whom I had not had some kind of personal contact. I did, however, make an exception for Anagarika Dharmapala, the first of my five great Buddhists, who died in India in 1933 when I was still a small boy living in Tooting, London. I feel justified in making this exception because I do have the sense that I lived with him for several weeks while composing my biography of him in 1952, having spent this time amongst the many volumes of his diaries.

Just one preliminary question remains to be cleared up, but it is quite an important one. How do we define a great Buddhist? Well, in the first place, great Buddhists have to be Buddhists. That is, they have to go for Refuge to the Three Jewels, to the Buddha, the

Dharma, and the Sangha. It is not enough in itself to be a great scholar of Buddhism, to be learned in Sanskrit and Pali, to make outstanding and original contributions to Buddhist studies.

It's not enough, either, to occupy a prominent position in a Buddhist organization. During my time in the East it was a recurring puzzle to me, when I came into contact with various Buddhist organizations, and met their presidents and secretaries, to discover that these dignitaries weren't actually Buddhists. So it is not enough to have a position of influence in the Buddhist world. Nor of course is it enough to have been born into a position of influence in the Buddhist world – to have been born into a Buddhist royal family, say.

Moreover, a great Buddhist is not just a great individual with Buddhist leanings. To be a great Buddhist, one would have to possess at least some of the characteristically Buddhist qualities to an eminent degree. Great Buddhists possess not just a little bit of *metta*, not just an occasional burst of *virya*, not just the beginnings of *prajna*. They have, we may say, at least some of these qualities 'in spades'.

Naturally, it goes without saying that they have, too, the basic human virtues – straightforward kindness and awareness of the needs of others, an integrated personality, self-knowledge, and so on – and these also to an eminent degree. One can't be a great – or even a good – Buddhist, without being a great or good human being.

Besides having at least some of these virtues, they should deploy them in their life and work in such a way as to influence many other people, especially many other Buddhists. Thus a great Buddhist contributes to the making of Buddhist history. Furthermore, a great Buddhist is a paradigmatic figure, providing a model or an example for other Buddhists, both when alive and after death. That is, he or she functions as a source of permanent inspiration and guidance for other Buddhists.

Not all the five here could be said to be equally great – though it is difficult to compare them very accurately in that way as they were great in very different ways. And I must also say that I personally don't necessarily agree with everything that each of them said or did or wrote. But they were all undoubtedly great in the sense that I have defined.

Finally, in our definition of terms, we come to 'twentieth century'. Strictly speaking, from a Buddhist point of view we should perhaps be talking about the 'twenty-fifth century' (i.e. after the Buddha's Enlightenment) – which concluded in 1956–7CE – rather than the twentieth century (i.e. after the birth of Christ). But never mind. 'Twentieth century' can be taken simply as convenient shorthand for 'more or less within living memory'. The first four of our great Buddhists were, in fact, all born in the nineteenth century, though they did most, if not all, their significant work for Buddhism in the twentieth.

My concern in these biographical sketches is not so much with the everyday biographical details – what they used to have for breakfast, say. It is rather with the significance of their lives for us, living as we do in the fresh wake of their achievements, and in something of the same twentieth century world as they did.

Anagarika Dharmapala

Dharmapala, the future 'Lion of Lanka' as he came to be called, was born in 1864 in Colombo, Sri Lanka – except that here we must call this island 'Ceylon', because that is the name it had in those days. His father was the proprietor of a furniture manufacturing business, so he had a solid, middle-class background; and his parents were good, pious Buddhists, so one might have thought that he would have had a solid, Buddhist background as well.

However, he was christened 'David' – his name was David Hewavitarne. And from the time he was five until eight, and again from ten to eighteen, he attended a series of Christian schools, both Catholic and Protestant. So this calls for some explanation. Why did his pious Buddhist parents send him to Christian schools?

The reason is simply that they had no choice. Ceylon had been a British colony since 1802, and before that, between 1505 and 1796, large parts of the island had been ruled first by the Portuguese and then by the Dutch. The result was that Buddhism and Buddhist culture at the time of Dharmapala's birth were at a very low ebb in Ceylon. In fact, it was not possible to be a Buddhist at all – at least, not officially. Children of Buddhist parents had to be taken for registration of their birth to a church – either Catholic or Protestant – and there given a Christian name. Otherwise, according to a law which was not repealed until 1884, the child would be illegitimate and unable to inherit property. And all education beyond primary level was in the hands of the missionaries.

So by the time he was in his early teens, Dharmapala knew by heart four complete books of the Old Testament, all four Gospels, and the Acts of the Apostles. However, he never lost faith in the Dharma. And later on, when Dharmapala came to the West as quite a celebrity and engaged in what we would call today 'inter-faith dialogue', Christians would sometimes regret that he knew their religion quite so intimately.

Dharmapala picked up a basic understanding of Buddhism at home, and being unusually argumentative, even for an adolescent boy, he used to get into trouble with his teachers for the persistence with which he picked away at inconsistencies in Christian doctrine. A much more serious offence, however, was his insistence on celebrating Wesak, the festival in honour of the Buddha's attainment of Enlightenment. At that time, of course, it wasn't a public holiday. Christmas was a public holiday, Easter was a public holiday – Wesak wasn't.

But when Dharmapala was in his early teens he realized that as a Buddhist he ought to celebrate Wesak, and in order to do this he would have to be given the day off school. So he went to the headmaster and asked to have the day off in order to celebrate the most important festival in the Buddhist calendar. Unsurprisingly, the headmaster said 'No'. Equally unsurprisingly, Dharmapala took his umbrella, walked out of the school, and simply didn't turn up for school the next day. He celebrated Wesak, and the following day was soundly thrashed. And this little drama was enacted between Dharmapala and his headmaster once a year for three consecutive years. This was how obstinate and determined he was, even as a boy.

We know a lot of details about Dharmapala's life, even before he became well-known, because he kept a diary more or less from the time he left school until his death in 1933. He also wrote some memoirs later on in life, and in these we find described another incident from his schooldays that shows a deeper side to his character.

It so happened that one of his schoolfellows died, and the corpse was laid out in the school. The teachers apparently invited the students to gather round the dead body of the boy and offer up prayers, and Dharmapala joined them. But as he looked around, a question came into his mind. He asked himself 'Why are they praying?' And as he continued to look at the faces of his schoolfellows, at the faces of the teachers, the answer came to him quite clearly that they were afraid; they were afraid of death. This was why they were praying. He saw that prayer – petitionary prayer – was born of fear. And from that day onward he had no temptation to pray in that sort of way.

This uppish, confrontational teenager, however, was also a rather dreamy lover of poetry, reading widely in English literature, especially the Romantics, and particularly Shelley. He read Keats and Shelley constantly. And this poetic streak went in counterpoint with marked mystical and ascetic tendencies.

Fortunately for this idealistic youth, things were changing, even in colonial Ceylon, and the tide was beginning to turn in

Buddhism's favour. In 1875 in New York, Madame Blavatsky and Colonel Olcott had founded the Theosophical Society. They were both very sympathetic to what they understood of Buddhism, and in 1880 they arrived in Ceylon, declared themselves to be Buddhists, and publicly took the Refuges and Precepts from a prominent Sinhalese bhikkhu. This created a tremendous sensation from one end of the island to the other, because they were the first Europeans publicly to embrace Buddhism.

The Christian missionaries were understandably very upset, and they continued to be upset because Colonel Olcott took rather a liking to Ceylon. He stayed on and devoted himself to the cause of Buddhist education, eventually setting up more than 300 Buddhist schools, some of which are still in existence. Sri Lankans still celebrate his work on 'Olcott Day'.

As for the still very young Dharmapala, he helped Colonel Olcott in his work, particularly by acting as his translator. Dharmapala also became quite close to Madame Blavatsky. In his late teens, he had wanted to study occultism, as so many Theosophists did, but Madame Blavatsky advised him to follow a very different course. She advised him to study Pali and to work for the good of humanity – which is what he did. And it was at this time that he changed his name from David to Dharmapala (meaning 'the Guardian of the Dharma').

In 1891 he paid his first visit to the holy places of northern India and found them in a shockingly neglected condition. Some of them were no more than ruins. This should not really have been any cause for surprise because Buddhism had disappeared from India several centuries before. Whatever of Buddhism that had not been absorbed by Hinduism had been destroyed by Muslim invaders.

The ancient Maha Bodhi Temple at Bodh Gaya, the most sacred of all the Buddhist holy places, had been restored by General Sir Alexander Cunningham. However, there was no one to look after the place, and when Dharmapala arrived there he was profoundly saddened by its desolate aspect. He sought out the Vajrasana, or 'Diamond Throne', the carved black marble slab that marks the spot where the Buddha, according to tradition, actually sat when he attained supreme Enlightenment, and bowing down before it he touched the edge with his forehead. And as he did so he was seized with a sudden inspiration. He would stay and look after the place until Buddhist monks could arrive and take over. At the age of 29 he had found his life's work.

It was not going to be as straightforward as he had thought it would be. Legally, the temple belonged to a Hindu monk, who was not pleased to have Dharmapala there, and at one point even had him thrown out and beaten up. Out of this ensued a long legal battle, which Dharmapala finally lost in 1906. Meanwhile, however, Dharmapala founded the Maha Bodhi Society to help him in his work. Initially, this work comprised the task of restoring Bodh Gaya to something of its former splendour; but the scope of the society's activities soon expanded to involve the promotion of Buddhism in India and eventually the development of Buddhism throughout the world. A natural extension of this work was to set up, in 1892, the *Maha Bodhi Journal*.

In 1893 Dharmapala was invited to attend the Parliament of World Religions in Chicago as representative of 'Southern Buddhism' – which was the term applied at that time to the Theravada. He was a great success. In fact some journalists paid him what they imagined to be the ultimate compliment, and compared him to Jesus. So by his early thirties he was already a global figure, and he continued to travel and give lectures and establish viharas around the world during the next forty years. At the same time he concentrated on establishing schools and hospitals in Ceylon and building temples and viharas in India. Amongst the most important of the temples he built was one at Sarnath, where the Buddha first taught the Dharma. Here, in 1933, when he was already a very sick man in a wheelchair, he was ordained a bhikkhu, and he died there in December of the same year, aged sixty-nine.

Dharmapala was a leading figure in initiating two outstanding features of Buddhism in the twentieth century. He was a great pioneer in the revival of Buddhism in India after it had been virtually extinct there for several centuries. And he was the first Buddhist in modern times to preach the Dharma in three continents, in Asia, in America, and in Europe.

Clearly, Dharmapala led a very active life. However, he invariably started his day, often before dawn, with two hours of meditation. In his younger days in Ceylon he had failed to find a meditation teacher; for various reasons, the practice of meditation there had simply died out. But in his twenties, he met a Burmese lay yogi who was able to give him some instruction. And the practice that we may say fuelled his life and work, was the metta bhavana, the cultivation of universal loving-kindness. So this is a vitally important aspect of his life. He wasn't simply a Buddhist activist, flitting from one Buddhist conference to another. His work for Buddhism sprang out of a deep experience of Buddhism – an experience that is enormously difficult to achieve without regular meditation.

One other significant aspect of his life was that he was the first anagarika – that is, a celibate, full-time worker for Buddhism – in modern times. He wasn't, until his last months, a bhikkhu – but he wasn't a layman in the ordinary sense either. It seems that he took a vow of celibacy or brahmacharya at the age of eight, and remained faithful to it all his life. And he also wore a yellow robe. However, it wasn't of the traditional bhikkhu pattern, and he didn't shave his head. He felt, so it would appear, that the observance of all the vinaya rules would have got in the way of his work, especially as he flew around the world.

Ultimately, the key to Dharmapala's life and work is before one's eyes wherever one opens his voluminous diaries. At the top of every alternate page he wrote: 'The only Refuge for him who aspires to true perfection is the Buddha alone.' This is what he reminded himself, every day of the year, year after year. Going for Refuge is the fundamental, decisive, definitive act of the Buddhist life. It is what makes us Buddhists, and it is what unites us all as Buddhists.

Alexandra David-Neel

Born in Paris in 1868, under the Emperor Napoleon III, Alexandra David-Neel died in southern France in 1969, under President Pompidou. She would have worn crinolines as a young woman, and she survived to see young women in mini-skirts. So this gives us some idea of the historical parameters of her very long life.

Her father was wealthy middle class – Protestant, socialist, and an ardent republican, whereas her mother was a Belgian Catholic, and an ardent supporter of the Belgian monarchy. Alexandra David – as she originally was – seems to have been very much closer to her father. Her mother had wanted a son, who would become a Catholic bishop; and a daughter was a bitter disappointment to her. So Alexandra grew up in these circumstances something of a tomboy. She went to various Catholic convents, but she remained a tomboy, and from the age of sixteen she started running away from home. She would come back again, but before long she was bicycling – this was in the 1880s – all the way to Spain. She also visited Holland, England, Italy, again all on her own, and still a teenager.

On her second visit to England she came in contact with Theosophists. She started reading up in the library of the British Museum the more alternative mystical traditions – Gnosticism, Catharism, and so on. And on her return to France she settled in Paris with a group of French Theosophists. She started to study Sanskrit, and in doing so came across the *Lalitavistara*, an imaginative and poetic, not to say legendary, life of the Buddha. However, this was not in fact her first contact with Buddhism. At the age of thirteen she had apparently come across one of the most ancient and beautiful Buddhist legends, the Jataka tale of how the Buddha, in one of his previous incarnations, had given his body to a starving tigress and her cubs. She had thought, at thirteen, that this was the most beautiful story she had ever heard.

Living in Paris she was also in contact with Buddhist art, because the Musée Guimet in Paris housed one of the most famous collections of oriental art in the world. There, one day, she stood before a magnificent Japanese Buddha image, joined her hands together, and bowed in salutation before it. She continued to study other religions, especially Hinduism, but she already regarded herself as a Buddhist.

At the age of twenty-one she came of age and inherited some money, which she spent on a trip to India, on her own, where she met maharajahs and swamis. She returned to Europe virtually penniless. She made a little money out of the occasional bit of journalism, but it wasn't enough. So she trained as a singer, and supported herself as a singer for seven years. She had quite a successful and rather colourful career as a singer, and in the course of it learned a lot about human nature. But her voice was evidently not very well trained because it started to deteriorate, so she decided, regretfully, that she would have to get married.

In 1904, at the age of thirty-six, Alexandra David married Philippe Neel, an aristocratic French engineer, then aged forty. They lived in French North Africa for a number of years, during which her beloved father died and she published her first book on Buddhism, called 'Buddhist modernism and the Buddhism of the Buddha'.

Alexandra David-Neel left for the East again in 1911, and she did not return for fourteen years. She travelled in Ceylon, India, Sikkim, Nepal, Japan, China, and Tibet, and continued her study of Buddhism. Not only that – she was putting what she studied into practice, which was unusual at that time. Not only was it unusual for a student of Buddhism to practise it; what she was doing was also unusual in another way. She met the thirteenth Dalai Lama – in exile in Kalimpong after an invasion by the Chinese – and he was astonished, on asking how she had become a Buddhist, to be told that it had been by reading books. He had never heard of such a thing.

In Sikkim, she met the Gomchen of Lhachen who was famous as a meditator and yogi (Gomchen meaning 'great meditator'). She became his disciple and spent two years there, practising meditation and studying Tibetan. She also adopted a Sikkimese boy – Lama Yongden as he afterwards became – and he remained with her for the rest of his life.

David-Neel's husband seems to have taken her extended absence very well. She wrote to him every day, so clearly she was fond of him, though equally clearly she could be fond of him only from a distance. In return he sent her money regularly – and she evidently needed plenty of it, to be frank. She usually travelled in some style, with a number of servants and a good deal of equipment.

There was one journey she took in rather less than grand style, and that was her famous journey to Lhasa. At that time foreigners were prohibited from entering Tibet, so she travelled in disguise. Her only companion was Yongden, who took the part of a travelling lama, with herself as his old mother. They were four months travelling on foot. They travelled through China to approach Lhasa from the north-east, crossing vast deserts, scaling lofty mountains and braving bandits, starvation, and landslides to reach their destination. They spent two months in Lhasa and David-Neel subsequently wrote 'The Journey of a Parisienne to Lhasa'.

In 1925 she returned to France with Yongden and settled in the Alps of Provence, at Digne. By now she was a rather famous elderly lady, giving lectures and writing books. She took a journey east just once more, in 1939, but this proved to be ill-timed. The Second World War broke out and the two of them were stranded in a small town in south-east Tibet called Darsendo (or Dhartsendo) for six years. Her husband was dead by the time they returned and Yongden died in 1955, but she continued to write. It was during this last period of her life that I had some contact with her. We exchanged letters and she contributed to magazines I was editing; and I noticed that her handwriting, despite her years, remained firm and clear.

Her life was noteworthy in three particular respects. First of all, she was one of the first Westerners to take Buddhism seriously – i.e. to take it as a way of life, not just as a subject for scholarly study. Secondly there was her readiness to defy convention, especially when convention stood in the way of the realization of her cherished ideals. Nowadays, when defying convention is often a meaningless convention in itself, it's difficult for us to realize how strong, how rigid, certain conventions were during her lifetime. For her, being unconventional took real courage. Thirdly and lastly, she showed what a really determined woman is capable of. Her life is thus an inspiration to all Buddhists, but perhaps to Buddhist women in particular.

B.R. Ambedkar

So far we have looked at individuals from wealthy, middle-class families. By contrast, Bimrao Ramji Ambedkar came from the very bottom of the social heap. He was born in 1891 at Mhow in central India into an Untouchable Hindu family, and this background to his life is very much what his career was about. To have any idea of what Ambedkar achieved one has to be clear about what this term 'Untouchable' really means.

Hindu society is divided into castes, with the Brahmins, the priestly caste, at the top, and the Shudras, or labouring caste, at the bottom, and others, with all sorts of subdivisions, in between. Having been born into a particular caste you can't get out of it – it is regarded as very wrong even to try. As for 'Untouchables', they are even lower than Shudras, and in a sense they are outside the caste system altogether. They are called 'Untouchables' because any contact with them pollutes so-called 'caste Hindus'. Even their shadow pollutes.

Traditionally, Untouchables lived in ghettoes of their own, outside the main community. They could engage only in very menial occupations such as removing night-soil, and they would serve the caste Hindu villagers in this way in return for a few scraps of food. They weren't allowed to enter Hindu temples or attend Hindu schools. They had no economic or political rights – they could not even own property. They were not allowed to better themselves in any way. Once an Untouchable, always an Untouchable – at least, so far as this life was concerned.

This system had been rigidly in force for a thousand years (and to all intents and purposes it still is in many areas). But when Ambedkar was born there were already faint signs that it was beginning to weaken. The rule of the British over India was no doubt unfortunate in many ways, but for the Untouchables it did have its advantages, because the British army accepted Untouchables into its ranks. In fact it had Untouchable regiments, and Ambedkar's father belonged to one of these. Members of these regiments were given a certain amount of education, and some, including Ambedkar's father, even became army schoolmasters.

With help and encouragement from his father, Ambedkar became a brilliant student, and at the age of seventeen was the first Untouchable to matriculate. He was given a scholarship by a liberal Indian prince, and eventually graduated in politics and economics. He studied further at Columbia University and then at the London School of Economics, and also qualified as a barrister. He returned to India in 1923, aged thirty-two, and took his place as one of the most highly gifted and qualified men in Indian public life.

However, he had not equipped himself so comprehensively for a political career out of self-interest. He never forgot that he himself was an Untouchable – nor was he allowed to. Many Indians continued to treat him as an Untouchable, and this was a source of great disappointment and bitterness to him; but it only hardened his resolve to devote his life to the uplift of his people. He founded newspapers, he started schools and colleges, he entered politics, he fought legal battles; and we may say that from 1923 until his death in 1956, the story of his life is inseparable from the history of modern India.

In 1927 Dr Ambedkar focused attention on the problems faced by his people by provoking the 'Chowdar Tank case'. In the town of Mahad in what is now Maharashtra state, Untouchables were not allowed to take water from this tank until 1927, when it was opened to them by the local municipality. Whether or not the Chowdar tank actually belonged to the municipality would be later contested. But meanwhile, Ambedkar held a conference of 3,000 Untouchables at Mahad, and at its conclusion led them to the edge of the tank to drink from it.

This may all seem a very tame business to us – a local dispute over who is allowed to use a water tank, and 3,000 people gathering together in order to dare to make use of what has been made available to them. But in India in those days it was a terrific, extraordinary, revolutionary thing to do. There was a furious reaction from the caste Hindus, and some of Ambedkar's followers were assaulted in one way or another for their impious – in the eyes of the caste Hindus – temerity. The Untouchables had, by drawing water from the tank, polluted it.

The question now was how to purify the tank again. Brahmins were called together, and they took 108 earthenware pots of water from the tank and mixed the water with curds, with milk, with cow-dung, and with cow's urine. Then the pots, with the water and the aforementioned 'purifying' elements, were put back in the tank and Vedic mantras were recited. In this way the tank was purified.

Naturally, a response to this insulting procedure was called for on the part of the Untouchables under Ambedkar, and it had to be an appropriate response, one that would get to the heart of the issue. In the same year, 1927, they burned the Manusmrti, or the 'Laws of Manu'. The significance of this book as a symbol resided in the fact that it is the source of all the laws regarding caste. It lays down who can eat with whom, who can marry whom, who can touch whom; and it also lays down how those who infringe those laws should be punished. Thus, for example, it is decreed that any Shudra who presumes to teach Brahmins their duty should have boiling oil poured into his mouth and into his ears. The burning of the Manusmrti had the desired effect. It shocked orthodox Hindus all over India, and it symbolized the repudiation by the Untouchables of the authority of the Hindu scriptures.

The man generally lauded nowadays as the great hero of this period in India, during the drive towards independence, is of course Mahatma Gandhi. But the Untouchables cannot see him in quite this idealized light. Gandhi was himself a caste Hindu who claimed to represent the Untouchables as well as caste Hindus, but the Untouchables did not recognize him in this role. They believed that only an Untouchable could safeguard their interests.

Gandhi had already agreed that Muslims, Christians, and Sikhs should have separate electorates, and Ambedkar argued that in a democratic India there should be separate electorates for Untouchables as well. This was because Untouchables did not want to be governed by caste Hindus. However, in 1932 Gandhi resisted Ambedkar's demands by going on one of his 'fasts to death', and during the period of the fast Ambedkar described himself as the most hated man in India. Gandhi did indeed come close to death, and in the end Ambedkar was forced to compromise. If Gandhi had fasted to death Ambedkar would have faced the prospect of the wholesale murder of Untouchables by caste Hindus.

In 1935 Ambedkar's wife died. He had married her very young, when he was sixteen and she just nine; only one of their five children had survived. By this time his political position was hardening. He no longer believed in the possibility of reform within Hinduism. He was convinced that the caste Hindus were not going to change their ways; they weren't going to treat the Untouchables as human beings. And in 1935 he made his famous declaration that though he had been born a Hindu, he would not die one.

In 1947 Ambedkar became Law Minister in the first government of the independent state of India, but he resigned from the Cabinet four years later because of fierce opposition from caste Hindus – even in the Cabinet – to his attempts to reform Hindu law. It was at about this time that I myself had some correspondence and then a series of meetings with him.

At the end of 1954 Ambedkar announced that he would devote the remainder of his life to the propagation of Buddhism in India. This was not a sudden decision. He had been a student of Buddhism for some time, and had known something about it ever since he was sixteen, when he had been given a copy of the Marathi translation of Edwin Arnold's *The Light of Asia*, a life of the Buddha in English verse (which had also been an early discovery and favourite of Dharmapala's).

Over the years Ambedkar had gradually become convinced that Buddhism was the best religion for himself and for the Untouchable community as a whole. There were various reasons for his choice, but the main ones were: firstly, that Buddhism did not conflict with the dictates of reason; secondly, that it did not condone man's inhumanity to man, and it certainly did not condone the caste system; and thirdly, that it was of Indian origin, it was not the product of a foreign culture.

So in 1956, in a ceremony at Nagpur in central India, Dr Ambedkar became a Buddhist – along with 380,000 of his followers. The conversions in Nagpur sparked off others all over India. It was the greatest event for Buddhism in India for many hundreds of years. Though these were 'mass conversions' the effect on the individuals who took part, who became Buddhists at that time, was profound. I used to ask people, months or even years afterwards, 'What difference has becoming a Buddhist meant for you?' And nine times out of ten they would reply, 'Now that I'm a Buddhist I feel free.' That seems to have been the most important aspect of the experience: a sense of freedom. They felt socially, psychologically, spiritually free.

Six weeks later, Ambedkar was dead, at the age of 64. I was in Nagpur at the time and I well remember the reaction of shock and grief that swept through the ex-Untouchable community. There were fears that the conversion movement would simply collapse. But happily it didn't collapse, and it continues to this day.

The significance of Dr Ambedkar's life and work is exceptionally profound and far-reaching. The problem he faced was how to lift up his people, socially, economically, educationally – in every respect. And he felt that the only overall solution to this problem was a change in religion. It wasn't enough just to reject Hinduism, just to leave the religion that generally condoned the caste system. Ambedkar himself was a deeply religious man; he believed that religion was essential to human life, that we cannot really live without it. So for him there was no question of pursuing, for instance, the communist option. He believed that a real social and economic revolution was possible only on the basis of a spiritual revolution.

It was for this reason that he inaugurated what we now call the 'Dhamma revolution'. This is not just a nominal change of religion, but a transformation of one's whole life in every aspect. It is not just individual transformation, but even collective transformation as well. This is the movement that Ambedkar set in motion. He showed that a change in religion, even in the midst of the twentieth century, could bring about a change for the better in the lives of millions of people.

The conversion movement in India is also of profound significance for Buddhism itself. Ambedkar was well aware that Buddhism had already disappeared once from India, and having revived it he didn't want it to disappear again. So he looked at why it had disappeared. He saw that one of the principal factors leading to its decline was the separation which had developed between the monks and the laity.

The monks lived together in monasteries, and in the course of centuries these monasteries became bigger and bigger, each in the end housing thousands of monks leading self-contained lives apart from the laity. So without much contact with the monks and without any lay ordination, the lay-people began to feel less and less like they themselves were Buddhists at all, and they came more and more under the influence of the Hindu brahmins. And this process was accelerated after the great monasteries were destroyed by Muslim invaders in the tenth, eleventh, and twelfth centuries. Thus eventually, the lay Buddhists were simply absorbed into the Hindu community. Buddhism disappeared from India, and only ruins marked what it once had been.

On the basis of this analysis of the decline and fall of Indian Buddhism, Ambedkar decided that there had to be ordination for lay-people corresponding to monastic ordination for monks. He called this lay ordination 'Dhammadiksha', and it consisted of two parts: first, taking the traditional Three Refuges and five precepts; and secondly – and this was quite new – taking twenty-two vows.

These twenty-two vows were devised by Ambedkar himself, and their purpose was to clearly and completely separate the new Buddhists from their old Hindu religion. They constituted an explicit renunciation of every vestige of Hinduism, of every Hindu practice, like, for example, offering animal sacrifices to gods and goddesses. These vows made it clear what it was to be a Hindu and what it was to be a Buddhist, and that it was not possible to be both. They helped to root out a very commonly held belief in India at this time that if you were a Buddhist you were necessarily also a Hindu, that Buddhism was an accretion on the main body of Hinduism. I myself remember a Hindu swami asking me after my ordination why I had not done the job properly and become a Hindu monk. 'Hinduism is like the great ocean,' he said, 'Buddhism is just a little stream.' In fact, any idea that Buddhism might be combined with another faith, whether Hinduism or Christianity, represents a serious confusion of thought. Dr Ambedkar thought that this principle was so important that it needed to be embodied in vows taken as part of the ordination ceremony.

The way it was done at Nagpur on 14 October 1956 was as follows: Dr Ambedkar took the Three Refuges and five precepts from U Chandramani, a very senior bhikkhu. After this, Ambedkar publicly recited his twenty-two vows. He then proceeded to administer the Refuges and precepts and the twenty-two vows himself to the 380,000 of his followers who were assembled there at Nagpur. In this way he established a very significant principle.

Ambedkar was initiated into Buddhism by a monk, but his followers were initiated into Buddhism by a layman. Thus the monk and the layman were placed, in a sense, on an equal footing. Dr Ambedkar was asserting the fact that it is Going for Refuge to the Three Jewels – the Buddha, the Dharma, and the Sangha – which makes one a Buddhist, not one's life-style. Going for Refuge is the primary act of a Buddhist; life-style – whether one is monk or lay – is secondary.

Lama Govinda

Lama Govinda was rather a mysterious figure – particularly when he was Ernst Lother Hoffman – which is the name with which he began life. We know very little about his early years. He was born in 1898 in Germany, into a middle-class family of partly Spanish descent, but his mother died when he was three, and he was brought up by her sister. He originally wanted to be a mining engineer, but developed an increasing interest in philosophy, especially Schopenhauer. He went on to study comparative religion, and Buddhism in particular, until, towards the end of the First World War, he was called up to spend two years in the German army.

After the war he took up residence in Capri, where began a very important period in his life. He studied Pali, he took up art and a bit of archaeological research, and he met an elderly German lady who became, for much of the rest of his life, a sort of foster-mother. He started practising meditation, and he started as well to make pastel drawings of the meditative states he experienced. So he was evidently already making the connection between meditation and art which would later be the subject of much of his thinking.

In 1928, aged thirty, Govinda moved to Ceylon – his foster-mother as well, of course. For a couple of years he studied Pali and Abhidhamma with the famous German bhikkhu, Nyanatiloka, during which period he took the name of Govinda and became an anagarika. He also visited Burma and researched cases of alleged recollection of previous lives, a subject he was always interested in.

His next move was to India, and at a Buddhist conference in Darjeeling he came into contact for the first time with Tibetan Buddhism, which thereafter exercised a compelling influence on his life and work. There are not many firm dates in what we know of Govinda's life, but about 1930 he settled – again with his foster-mother – in Ghoom near Darjeeling, where he met his Tibetan guru, the famous Tomo Geshe Rimpoche. During the next few years he was based partly in Ghoom and partly in Shantiniketan, the forest university established by Rabindranath Tagore a hundred miles north of Calcutta.

Govinda lectured, he wrote, he travelled – until in 1942 he was interned by the British because of his German descent. Conditions in the camp near Dehradun were very mild: he studied Chinese, he studied the I Ching, and he enjoyed the companionship of Nyanaponika, another German disciple of Nyanatiloka. After the war he returned to Ghoom and to Shantiniketan, and in 1947 he married a former student of his at Shantiniketan, Rati Petit, who became known as Li Gotami.

In 1948 they made their celebrated journey to Tsaparang in western Tibet, and they made it just in time, because within a year or two the Chinese had occupied the whole of Tibet. The two of them spent several months working in conditions of great hardship, sketching, and photographing ruined Buddhist temples and monasteries, and copying ancient frescoes.* They were greatly impressed, not so much by the religious life they found there as by the vastness of the open spaces, by the views, by the brilliant colours, by the light, and of course by the ancient art that they discovered.

In 1952 Govinda announced the formation of the Arya Maitreya Mandala, an organization through which he hoped to spread Buddhism, especially Tibetan Buddhism, in the West. Shortly afterwards, he and Li Gotami moved to Almora in the foothills of the western Himalayas, where they remained for the next twenty-five years, and where Govinda had the most creative phase of his career, producing at least two Buddhist literary classics: the semi-autobiographical *Way of the White Clouds*, documenting the journey to western Tibet; and *Foundations of Tibetan Mysticism*. In the sixties and seventies they made several trips to Europe and America, where there was a growing interest in Buddhism, and they spent their last years in San Francisco, where Govinda died in 1985, aged 87. Li Gotami died in India about three years later.

I personally got to know Lama Govinda really quite well. We discovered that we had a good deal in common, especially in our

* Lama Anagarika Govinda, *The Way of the White Clouds*, Rider, 1966.

approach to Buddhism. In a letter he wrote to me four days before he died he made a couple of points that seem to indicate what the overall direction of his life and work had been. Firstly: 'I'm a great admirer of Italian art and, like you, I always uphold the importance of European culture. Without knowing the roots of our own culture how can we absorb the essence of Buddhist culture?' And secondly: 'Now it is up to the next generation to take Buddhism out of the merely academic atmosphere and make it a living experience.'

Lama Anagarika Govinda always emphasized that intellectual understanding and the observance of rules wasn't enough, but that Buddhism could be made a living experience by means of meditation, together with ritual and particularly colour – colour in the full, literal sense – in the spiritual life. He also stressed the importance of what he called 'creative imagination' and thus the importance of art. As a meditator and an artist himself, he did not see these two activities as completely different. In fact, he saw a sort of parallelism between them. The way he put it was that in meditation we pass from the world of outward expression to the world of inner experience; and in art we pass from the world of inner experience to the world of outward expression.

Edward Conze

Ebehart Julius Dietrich Conze was born in London in 1904 of mixed German, French, and Dutch ancestry. His father belonged to the German landed aristocracy, and his mother to what he himself would have called the 'plutocracy'. His background was Protestant, though his mother became a Roman Catholic in later life. He seems to have had a rather bad relationship with his mother – like Alexandra David-Neel, though obviously for different reasons.

He was born in England simply because his father happened to be posted there as German Vice-Consul, but this meant that he had British nationality, should he ever need it (which he would). He was educated at various German universities and with a flair for languages picked up a command of fourteen of them, including Sanskrit, by the age of twenty-four. Like many other Europeans, he came into contact with Theosophy quite early on. But he also took up astrology. He took it seriously, remaining a keen astrologer all his life. And while still a young man, he wrote a very substantial book called *The Principle of Contradiction*. Apparently his mother said that she was not surprised he'd written such a book since he himself was a bundle of contradictions.

During the rise to power of Hitler, Conze found himself so strongly opposed to the Nazi ideology that he joined the Communist Party and even made a serious study of Marxist thought. It seems that for a while he was the leader of the communist movement in Bonn, and his life was consequently in some danger.

In 1933 he came to England, having earlier taken the precaution of renewing his British nationality, and he arrived at the age of twenty-nine, virtually without money or possessions. He supported himself by teaching German, and taking evening classes, and he became a member of the Labour Party. He met a lot of prominent figures and intellectuals in the Labour movement and was not impressed. He had, after all, been to a whole series of German universities. He met Trades Union leaders and he met Pandit Nehru and Krishna Menon of the India League and he was not impressed by any of them either. He was not easily impressed.

He became very active in the socialist movement in Britain, lecturing and writing books and pamphlets, until eventually he became disillusioned with politics. At the age of thirty-five he found himself in a state of intellectual turmoil and collapse. Even his marriage had failed. Indeed, in his memoirs he admits 'I am one of those unfortunate people who can neither live with women nor without them.'

At this point he discovered – or rather rediscovered – Buddhism. At the age of thirteen he had read *Gleanings in Buddha Fields* by Lafcadio Hearn, which I myself read in my own teens (and at the beginning of each chapter he would have read quotations from the *Diamond Sutra*, as if presaging his future life's work). However, Conze's first significant contact with Buddhism was at this midpoint in his life, at the beginning of the Second World War, and it was through the writings of D.T. Suzuki. They were literally his salvation.

After this there was no turning back. Conze devoted the rest of his life to Buddhism, and in particular to translating the Prajnaparamita or Perfection of Wisdom sutras, which are the fundamental scriptures of the Mahayana. But he wasn't just a scholar in the academic sense. During the war he lived on his own in a caravan in the New Forest, and he practised meditation, following very seriously the instructions given by Buddhaghosha in the *Visuddhimagga*, and achieving some degree of meditative experience.

After the war he moved to Oxford and re-married. In 1951 he brought out *Buddhism: Its Essence and Development*, a very successful book which is still in print. However, his real achievement over the following twenty years was to translate altogether more than thirty texts comprising the Prajnaparamita sutras, including of course two of the most well-known of all Buddhist texts, the *Diamond Sutra* and the *Heart Sutra*.

It was in connection with these translations that I myself came into contact with him. I started publishing his *Selected Sayings from the Perfection of Wisdom* in a magazine I was editing called *Stepping Stones* in about 1951. We corresponded, and when I came to England in 1964 we met a number of times and found that we agreed on quite a lot of issues.

In the sixties and seventies he lectured at several universities in the United States, and he went down well with the students. However, he was very outspoken, and gained the disapproval of the university authorities and some of his colleagues. With the combination of his communist past and his candid criticism of the

American involvement in Vietnam, he was eventually obliged to take his talents elsewhere. He died in 1979.

Dr Conze was a complex figure, and it is not easy to assess his overall significance. He was of course a Middle European intellectual refugee, fleeing from Germany before the war like so many others. But he wasn't at all representative of this dominant strain in twentieth century intellectual life, because he was very critical of many trends in modern thought. He was a self-confessed élitist, which is usually something people are ashamed of nowadays, but he wasn't ashamed of it at all. Indeed, he entitled his autobiography *Memoirs of a Modern Gnostic*, believing as he did that Gnosticism was essentially élitist. Nor did he approve of either democracy or feminism, which makes him a veritable ogre of 'political incorrectness'.

He is certainly representative of a whole pre-war generation in the West which became disillusioned with Marxism, especially with Marxism in its Soviet form. Where he differed from others was in the fact that he did not really lose his sense of faith. He did not simply become disillusioned while carrying on within the milieu he was familiar with. He transferred his uncompromising idealism from politics to Buddhism.

Dr Conze was one of the great Buddhist translators, comparable with the indefatigable Chinese translators Kumarajiva and Hsuan-tsang of the fifth and seventh centuries respectively. It is especially significant, I think, that as a scholar of Buddhism he also tried to practise it, especially meditation. This was very unusual at the time he started his work, and he was regarded then – in the forties and fifties – as being something of an eccentric. Scholars were not supposed to have any personal involvement in their subject. They were supposed to be 'objective'. So he was a forerunner of a whole new breed of Western scholars in Buddhism who are actually practising Buddhists.

This overview of some great Buddhist lives does not in any way provide a comprehensive view of the achievements of the great Buddhists of the twentieth century. For that, we would have to introduce many others. The thirteenth Dalai Lama, the Zen scholar and translator, D.T. Suzuki, Dr G.P. Malalasekera of Sri Lanka, Bhikkhu Buddhadasa of Thailand, the great Chinese Ch'an meditation master the Venerable Hsu Yun, and the great Chinese abbot Tai Hsu are just some of them.

However, I hope I have been able to suggest what we may gain, as Buddhists, from reading, studying, reflecting, and meditating on the lives, the biographies, and memoirs of Buddhists who have lived, in one way or another, truly inspiring lives. They enable us to see Buddhism being actually lived. Purely doctrinal studies – good and necessary though they may be – sometimes give us the impression that Buddhism is rather remote from our own twentieth century lives. Biographies help to redress this balance. After all, Buddhism began with lives; it didn't begin with books. Buddhism began with the lives of the Buddha and his Enlightened disciples.

While preparing these sketches of great Buddhists I noticed two things. I noticed first of all that the five were all very different. They had very different characters and they grew up in very different circumstances. In many ways they did very different things. But they were all great Buddhists. This is very important. It reminds us that though we are all Buddhists, though we all go for Refuge, we don't all have to be the same; we don't have to live in the same way; we don't have to do the same things. This is because what unites us is more important than what divides us.

The second thing I noticed was that there were certain qualities which, despite their differences, all five seemed to possess. To begin with, they were all very single-minded. Once they had discovered their purpose in life, they never wavered. Then, they were all characterized by fearlessness. They were also all unconventional. And they were self-motivated. They were autonomous individuals, they 'did their own thing', they went their own way, sometimes in the face of tremendous opposition. They were all true individuals.

In short, they were all heroes, in the best sense of the term. We need to cherish our heroes and heroines. We need to admire them, we need to cherish their memory, we need to rejoice in their merits. We need to appreciate that our great Buddhists, whether of the twentieth or any other century, are among our greatest and most precious possessions.

Further Reading

Ambedkar

B.R. Ambedkar, *Annihilation of Caste*, Bheem Patrika Publications, Jullundur 1978
Dhananjay Keer, *Dr Ambedkar, Life and Mission*, Popular Prakashan PVT, Bombay 1971
Terry Pilchick, *Jai Bhim! Dispatches from a Peaceful Revolution*, Windhorse, Glasgow, and Parallax, California, 1988
Sangharakshita, *Ambedkar and Buddhism*, Windhorse, Glasgow 1989

Dharmapala

Anagarika Dharmapala, *Return to Righteousness: A Collection of Speeches, Essays and Letters of the Anagarika Dharmapala*, ed. Ananda Guruge, The Anagarika Dharmapala Birth Centenary Committee, Ministry of Education and Cultural Affairs, Ceylon 1965
Sangharakshita, *Flame in Darkness: The Life and Sayings of Anagarika Dharmapala*, Triratna Grantha Mala, Poona 1995

Conze

Edward Conze, *Buddhism: Its Essence and Development*, Bruno Cassirer, Oxford 1957
Edward Conze, *Buddhist Wisdom Books: The Diamond and the Heart Sutra*, Unwin Hyman, London 1988
Edward Conze, *Further Buddhist Studies: Selected Essays by Edward Conze*, Bruno Cassirer, Oxford 1975
Edward Conze, *Memoirs of a Modern Gnostic* (2 vols.), Samizdat, 1979
Edward Conze, *Thirty Years of Buddhist Studies: Selected Essays by Edward Conze*, Bruno Cassirer, Oxford 1967

David-Neel

Alexandra David-Neel, *Magic and Mystery in Tibet*, HarperCollins, London 1992
Alexandra David-Neel, *My Journey to Lhasa*, Virago, London 1988
Ruth Middleton, *Portrait of an Adventurer*, Shambhala, Boston/London 1989

Govinda

Lama Anagarika Govinda, *Creative Meditation and Multi-Dimensional Consciousness*, Theosophical Publishing House, Wheaton, Illinois 1990
Lama Anagarika Govinda, *The Way of the White Clouds*, Rider, London 1995
Ken Winkler, *A Thousand Journeys: The Biography of Lama Anagarika Govinda*, Element, 1990

Also

Stephen Batchelor, *The Awakening of the West: The Encounter of Buddhism and Western Culture*, HarperCollins, London 1995
Sangharakshita, *Facing Mount Kanchenjunga: An English Buddhist in the Eastern Himalayas*, Windhorse, Glasgow 1991
Sangharakshita, *In the Sign of the Golden Wheel: Indian Memoirs of an English Buddhist*, Windhorse, Birmingham 1996
(Forthcoming) Sangharakshita, *The Rainbow Road*, Windhorse, Birmingham 1997

The Windhorse symbolizes the energy of the enlightened mind carrying the Three Jewels – the Buddha, the Dharma, and the Sangha – to all sentient beings.

Buddhism is one of the fastest growing spiritual traditions in the Western world. Throughout its 2,500-year history, it has always succeeded in adapting its mode of expression to suit whatever culture it has encountered.

Windhorse Publications aims to continue this tradition as Buddhism comes to the West. Today's Westerners are heirs to the entire Buddhist tradition, free to draw instruction and inspiration from all the many schools and branches. Windhorse publishes works by authors who not only understand the Buddhist tradition but are also familiar with Western culture and the Western mind.

For orders and catalogues contact:

WINDHORSE PUBLICATIONS
UNIT 1-316 THE CUSTARD FACTORY
GIBB STREET
BIRMINGHAM B9 4AA
UK

WINDHORSE PUBLICATIONS (USA)
14 HEARTWOOD CIRCLE
NEWMARKET
NEWHAMPSHIRE 03857
USA

Windhorse Publications is an arm of the Friends of the Western Buddhist Order, which has more than sixty centres on four continents. Through these centres, members of the Western Buddhist Order offer regular programmes of events for the general public and for more experienced students. These include meditation classes, public talks, study on Buddhist themes and texts, and 'bodywork' classes such as t'ai chi, yoga, and massage. The FWBO also runs several retreat centres and the Karuna Trust, a fundraising charity that supports social welfare projects in the slums and villages of India.

Many FWBO centres have residential spiritual communities and ethical businesses associated with them. Arts activities are encouraged too, as is the development of strong bonds of friendship between people who share the same ideals. In this way the FWBO is developing a unique approach to Buddhism, not simply as a set of techniques, less still as an exotic cultural interest, but as a creatively directed way of life for people living in the modern world.

If you would like more information about the FWBO please write to:

LONDON BUDDHIST CENTRE
51 ROMAN ROAD
LONDON
E2 0HU
UK

ARYALOKA
14 HEARTWOOD CIRCLE
NEWMARKET
NEWHAMPSHIRE 03857
USA

Also from Windhorse

SANGHARAKSHITA
AMBEDKAR AND BUDDHISM

The remarkable and stirring story of Dr Bhimrao Ramji Ambedkar, lawyer, politician, and educationalist, who, in 1956, started the most important social revolution occurring in India today: the conversion, from Hinduism to Buddhism, of millions of Indians wishing to escape the degradation of the caste system.

Sangharakshita knew Ambedkar personally, and himself played an important part in the 'Mass Conversion Movement' that Ambedkar set in motion. In this book he explores the historical, religious, and social background to that movement, and assesses the considerable contribution made by Ambedkar to the spiritual tradition in which he placed his trust.

179 pages
ISBN 0 904766 28 4
£5.95/$11.95

SANGHARAKSHITA
FLAME IN DARKNESS: THE LIFE AND SAYINGS OF ANAGARIKA DHARMAPALA

Buddhism is spreading throughout the world as never before in the course of its long and glorious history. One of the greatest figures to contribute to the spread of the Buddha's teaching in this century is undoubtedly Anagarika Dharmapala.

In this book, Sangharakshita gives a very moving account of the Anagarika's life, an example that cannot fail to inspire all those who consider themselves Buddhists.

Published by Triratna Grantha Mala, Poona, 1995
144 pages
£4.99

TERRY PILCHICK (NAGABODHI)
JAI BHIM! DISPATCHES FROM A PEACEFUL REVOLUTION

In the 1940s and 50s, Bhimrao Ramji Ambedkar – champion of India's 60,000,000 'Untouchables' – could have launched a violent struggle for freedom. Instead he asked his people to find dignity, strength, and prosperity by converting to Buddhism.

There are now millions of new Buddhists in India; they still meet and part with the words, 'Jai Bhim!' – 'Victory to Bhimrao Ambedkar'.

Travelling around the Buddhist localities, meeting and living with Ambedkar's modern followers, Terry Pilchick gained an intimate impression of the unique revolution they are building. In a colourful, moving account, he allows us to witness the revolution for ourselves.

240 pages
ISBN 0 904766 36 5
£5.95/$12.50